HOPE FOR HURTING HEARTS:

CHALLENGE FOR HUNGRY HEARTS:

Quotes on faith, prayer & revival taken from the sayings of renowned author & evangelist,
Dr. E. A. Johnston

Including his internationally known sermon:
"America: Revival or Ruin"

E. A. Johnston, Ph.D.

"HOPE FOR HURTING HEARTS:
A CHALLENGE FOR HUNGRY HEARTS"

By Dr. E. A. Johnston
© Copyright 2025

ISBN: 979-8-9921926-9-8

Printed in the United States of America

Formatting and Publishing by
The Old Paths Publications, Inc
TOP@theoldpathspublications.com
www.theoldpathspublications.com
January 2025

COVER PHOTO:

The Author is preaching from the pulpit of the Old South First Presbyterian Church in Newburyport, MA. The sign behind him reads: "Underneath this pulpit are deposited the remains of the Rev. George Whitefield."

DEDICATION

This book is dedicated to the memory of my Pastor, colleague, and friend: Dr. Adrian Rogers, of whom every time I was with him, he made me think of Jesus.

E. A. Johnston
March 2025

TABLE OF CONTENTS

8

INTRODUCTION

"Whenever I get too big for my britches, God puts me on His grill and barbeques me!"

E. A. Johnston

These various "little sayings" of mine have sprung through the years of a deep well of heartache and heartbreak; tragedy and trial; adversity and affliction, correction and growth, valleys and mountaintops, that I have personally experienced as a Christian.

It has been said that the role of a preacher is to comfort the "afflicted" and afflict the "comfortable." These sayings provided here achieve those two objectives.

It is my prayer that the compilation of these "sayings" can be for you, as they have been for me, both a catharsis and a tonic for the soul, as well as a comfort and a challenge to go deeper with God. May these sayings be like red hot coals on the altar of your heart as they ignite your sweetheart love for Jesus.

God gets serious with those who get serious with Him. As you read this little book may God's presence stir your heart to believe you can do great things for Him!

Evangelist & Author, E. A. Johnston

COLLECTION ONE:
SAYINGS ON GRIEF & TRAGEDY

WHEN THE DEVIL WENT DOWN TO MEMPHIS

"After my wife's tragic suicide, as I sat in the police station waiting room the TV was turned to a vile talk show where the topic was perverted sex. And as I placed my elbows on my knees and my hands over my ears to drown out the foul language on TV, I sensed a visitor beside me on the little couch. It was the enemy of my soul. I am convinced until I die that Satan physically visited me that terrible day and was sitting beside me mocking me in my tragedy."

E. A. Johnston

THE GOD OF COMFORT

"There are times when God doesn't make sense; but it is during 'those times' that we can sense Him."

E. A. Johnston

"You don't lose your faith because of tragedy; it is your faith that gets you through the tragedy."

E. A. Johnston

"When the world stands against you and friends desert you—you have a Faithful Friend who will stand by your side. Jesus will never let you down or ever let you go--He is with you to the end."

E. A. Johnston

HOW GOD BUILDS FAITH

"Faith is not built beneath calm, sunny skies but formed during dark, tempest tossed nights. Faith doesn't grow like a flower in a garden rather, it is often hammered out on the anvil of adversity and shaped in the furnace of affliction."

E. A. Johnston

COLLECTION TWO:

SAYINGS ON GOD'S FAITHFULNESS & OUR FAITH

Romans 8:39 declares: 'Nor height, nor depth, nor any other creature, shall be able to separate us from the love of God, which is in Christ Jesus our Lord.'

"The love of God in Christ Jesus our Lord spoken of here, is a love much deeper than the oceans, far higher than the galaxy of stars, more invincible than any hellish host against us, more steady than the sunrise on the horizon, and much greater than any human love of the heart---for it is a love existing before the world began, an everlasting love that sent a Saviour to die upon a cross for our sins, because 'he loved me and gave himself for me'; it is the unsearchable and unfathomable love of our Faithful Friend who will never let us down or ever let us go for He loves us to the end with an endless everlasting love."

E. A. Johnston

"Faith and obedience go hand in hand like biscuits and gravy, one compliments the other."

E. A. Johnston

"Faith is the car battery that starts the engine of obedience."

E. A. Johnston

"Faith is going out on a limb for God when all your other limbs are exposed."

E. A. Johnston

"God is looking for faith, Satan is looking for victims, and the church is looking for new members."

E. A. Johnston

"God is looking for the Moses, who will take time to turn aside and encounter Him to experience change; so God can send him to deliver a nation."

E. A. Johnston

"Jesus is my Faithful Friend but can He say that about me?

E. A. Johnston

"Can our life be explained on normal terms or are we an astonishment to many?

E. A. Johnston

"God is looking for faith—He demands obedience."

E. A. Johnston

"A believer is full of Jesus, an unbeliever is full of the Devil, and the world is full of fools."

E. A. Johnston

"When Jesus was here in His earthly ministry, as He passed through towns and villages, those who encountered Him experienced change. Have you encountered Him and have you experienced change?"

E. A. Johnston

"Jesus is not only worthy, He is worth it. He is worth selling all for and losing all for so He may be gained."

E. A. Johnston

FAITH IS

"Faith is believing what God says over whatever everybody else says; Faith is hope in the Blessed Hope when you have no hope; Faith is believing God's promises come Hell or high water; Faith is believing God's gonna do what He said he'd do; Faith is activated by obedience; Faith is going out on a limb for God when the limb is hanging by a thread and a storm is coming; Faith is doing what God told you to do when family and friends told you not to do it; Faith is believing God can still do the impossible in your impossible situation; Faith is facing adversity head on when your head is already on the chopping block; Faith is believing God can do the extraordinary with the ordinary; Faith is believing God is bigger than my biggest problem; Faith is believing God will answer prayer when prayer is your only answer;

Faith is leaving the safety of the boat to go out on the water because Jesus is out on the water; Faith is standing on the promises of God when there's nothing left to stand on but the promises of God."

E. A. Johnston

"Faith is looking with the eye of faith through the visible to see the invisible to grab the impossible."

E. A. Johnston

"God's Word is true and God is true to His Word."

E. A. Johnston

"God is the same God today as He was working miracles in Bible. We could see Him move in that same capacity today if we could 'only believe'."

E. A. Johnston

THE TRIAL OF FAITH GROWS OUR FAITH AND MAKES US MORE FRUITFUL

"God builds faith when it is tried. This is done through the Divine process of reducing and refining. Gold must be refined in the furnace of affliction to be reduced to its purity. A branch must be pruned back with a sharp knife and decreased before it can produce more fruit. It we want our faith to grow in further usefulness to God, then we must submit both to the Refiner's fire and the Divine pruning knife."

E. A. Johnston

COLLECTION THREE:

SAYINGS ON PRAYER & CHRISTIAN LIVING

"If you are praying for a loved one to be saved, or praying for a deliverance from your adverse circumstances and nothing seems to be happening in regard to that answered prayer—then take heart and be encouraged for there is no expiration of a prayer, for a prayer once made has wings, a life and a force that reach far into the future and into eternity—all for the glory of God."

E. A. Johnston

"The greatest need in our Land today is a prophet. A man sent from God. God's man who will stand in the gap between heaven and earth, between mortal man and Almighty God. A holy man who is so wholly sold out to God, so intoxicated with Christ, and so consumed with eternity that his very footprints leave a smoky trail of the lingering fire of God. A man whose desperate life of prayer has left fingerprints on the horns of the altar in glory. A man whose emboldened prayers of faith and Enoch-like walk with God moves mountains of resistance and proves that the God of the Bible is alive and interested in the most minute requests of man."

E. A. Johnston

"The church today operates on money and manpower, but in former times it operated on prayer and Holy Ghost power."

E. A. Johnston

DESPERATE PRAYERS

'And Hannah prayed' (1 Samuel 2:1) are three of the most power-packed words found on prayer in our Bible, for when Hannah prayed she laid hold of God in desperation and determination as she confessed her utter necessity of Him to give her a man child. This is how prophets are born—born out of the desperate prayers of heart-burdened parents crying out to God for their children to know God and be used of Him."

E. A. Johnston

"God will always raise up an Elijah whose prayers impact a sleeping nation. The Church in each generation has had individuals who live upon their knees, whose prayers reach heaven with a holy violence. India had her 'praying Hyde'; China her Hudson Taylor; England her Puritans; Scotland her Covenanters; America her fiery E. M. Bounds; voices which gained the attention of the Throne-room, startled angels, and shook the gates of hell making even the demons quake and tremble with their desperate prayers."

E. A. Johnston

"There can be only one answer to the question, 'Why has the church lost her power?' The answers lies in the reality that the Church has forsaken the Third Person of the Trinity, replacing Him with programs, money and man-centered methodologies. Our reliance is one of self, rather than reliance upon the Holy Spirit to empower us to pray, preach, and witness with an enduement from on High.”

E. A. Johnston

LIVING FOR ETERNITY

“If we are not living for Christ and eternity, what are we doing here?”

E. A. Johnston

“What is my life that I should keep it selfishly for me? I choose to lose it so completely and have it found in Thee.”

E. A. Johnston

“Self is a tyrant that if not dethroned, will remain enthroned.”

E. A. Johnston

“If you didn’t live your life for eternity, you sure will have a long time to think about it.”

E. A. Johnston

We read in 1 Corinthians 11-15, ‘For other foundation can no man lay than that is laid, which is Jesus Christ. Now if any man build upon this foundation gold, silver, precious stones, wood, hay, stubble; every man's work shall be made manifest: for the day shall declare it, because it shall be revealed by fire; and the fire shall try every man's work of what sort it is. If any man's work abide which he hath built thereupon, he shall receive a reward. If any man's work shall be burned, he shall suffer loss; but he himself shall be saved; yet so as by fire.'

"At the Bema seat of Christ, will the works of my life as a believer end up as gold, silver and precious stones reflecting the Lord of glory? Or will I stand there knee-deep in the ashes of a wasted life and lean over to scoop up those ashes and attempt to press them in His nail-pierced Hands!"

E. A. Johnston

"If God gave you an eraser, what part of your life would you erase?"

E. A. Johnston

"If you're not born from above and washed in the Blood, you'll bust Hell wide open when you die—even if you are the Chairman of the deacons."

E. A. Johnston

"If you've been suffering from 'Elevator Christianity', where one day you are up on the top floor enjoying the penthouse suite, and the next day incredibly you are down in the dumps in the basement of defeat, then it's time to get off the elevator and climb the stairs."

E. A. Johnston

"When we are dead and gone will our memory be a fragrant aroma of Christ Jesus?"

E. A. Johnston

"Adrian Rogers made me think of Jesus. Every time I was with him I felt I was in the presence of Jesus. Who do you make people think of?"

E. A. Johnston

"Are we willing to be decreased so Jesus can be increased in our life, or are we crowding Him out so we can be more visible?"

E. A. Johnston

"King Solomon was a man who had had it all, seen it all, and had done it all, and he was sick of it all—until he made God his all-in-all."

E. A. Johnston

"If there is a literal Hell that fills every minute with the damned, why are you wasting minutes by not spreading the Gospel in your community? What excuse will you give Jesus on That Day?"

E. A. Johnston

"If you end your days and you failed to risk everything for Christ and the Gospel, it will be too late then."

E. A. Johnston

"A disciple means 'learner'. Jesus is looking for those followers of His who are teachable."

E. A. Johnston

"If Jesus held nothing back at Calvary to die for our sins, how can we hold anything back from Him?"

E. A. Johnston

"I was lost and Jesus found me, I was filthy and He cleansed me, I was a rebel and He conquered me, I was crooked and He straightened me, I was empty and He filled me, I was broken and He used me."

E. A. Johnston

"God is looking for the person He can use to be a means of blessings to others. The criteria are: availability, obedience, and faith."

E. A. Johnston

"Be willing to be reduced to nothing, so He can be everything through you."

E. A. Johnston

"If Jesus told His disciples to tarry in the city until they were endued with power from on high, the we should do the same. We should not move one skinny inch for God without the power of God upon us."

E. A. Johnston

"Our fruitfulness to God depends on four things: yieldedness, obedience, holiness, usefulness. Without yieldedness there is no obedience; without obedience there is no holiness; without holiness there is no useful-ness."

E. A. Johnston

"When God comes in, everything else must go out. God can use an empty cup that He can fill."

E. A. Johnston

"Absolute surrender means ab-solute dependence."

E. A. Johnston

"Once you step out on the water by faith and like Peter get a taste of the supernatural—the last thing you want to do is go back to the safety of the boat."

E. A. Johnston

"Satan came against Jesus at the entrance and exit of His earthly ministry; if the Devil can't get you in the beginning, he will try to get you in the end. Sadly, some promising servants play footsie free with Satan and end up with a sad ending, a ruined testimony and a wrecked ministry."

E. A. Johnston

"When we are not exercising our graces we are slumbering in spiritual decay. Had Noah exercised his graces more than guzzling his grapes, he would not have lain naked in his tent sleeping off his hangover. Had Lot been exercising his graces more than worrying about his skin, he would have been more aware to the depravity of his daughters. Had David been exercising his graces by leading a battle for God rather than reclining on his couch he would have avoided the nakedness of Bathsheba and following the lustful inclinations of his heart."

E. A. Johnston

COLLECTION FOUR:

SAYINGS ON REVIVAL AND SPIRITUAL AWAKEING

MEN WITH HEARTS ON FIRE

"God's eyes are continually searching the earth for those rare individuals of 'whom the world was not worthy'. Men like Moses and John the Baptist; Luther and Calvin; Wesley and Whitefield; Finney and Moody. Men who live in a different atmosphere than other mortals; men who have annihilated self with the Cross and whose lives are broken alabaster boxes from which fragrances arise to the heavens from the broken pieces of selflessness, self-sacrifice, and self-crucifixion. God is always on the 'look out' for such men."

E. A. Johnston

"We need God-called preachers anointed with the Holy Ghost who preach 'searching sermons' with the force of volcano where every word falls with the weight of a hammer, burns the conscience like a fire, and cuts with conviction like a knife."

E. A. Johnston

"Samuel hewed old rotten King Agag to pieces because prideful King Saul was derelict in his duty to do the same. As preachers, our sermons should cut men to pieces, bringing conviction of sin and showing them their need of a Savior for sin."

E. A. Johnston

"Why could Moody hold ten thousand at a time for a month at a time in the chief capitals of England and Scotland? As an uneducated man, Moody could barely speak English well, yet scholars hung on his every word. How could Whitefield hold thirty thousand hearers in the open air in bitter cold, rainy, mornings for two hours at a time holding them spellbound while shivering? Men like Whitefield and Moody simply wouldn't leave the Devil alone. They "went after" men in hedges and fields and bars and street corners to flush them out so they could hear of the love of a Redeemer who died on a bloody Cross for sinners and a wretch like them."

E. A. Johnston

"Modern evangelism offers Jesus like a free stick of chewing gum, and people accept our 'little Jesus' and chew on him for a while until the flavor goes out of their religion."

E. A. Johnston

"Asahel Nettleton was the primary leader of the time period known in America as The Second Great Awakening. His sermons were both a shotgun that hit you all over and a rifle aimed at the very conscience of men. Strong men would tremble when he came to town because they knew a revival of religion would soon follow and expose their rotten hearts. While preaching the evening service in a church in Pittsfield, MA in 1828 he chose for his text, Genesis 19. It was said by an eyewitness that his descriptions of the burning of Sodom were so graphic and unsettling that it 'turned the heads of the congregation toward the windows to witness the conflagration.'"

E. A. Johnston

WE NEED MEN LIKE THESE

"The Apostle Paul, Luther, Wesley, Whitefield, Knox, Edwards, Finney, Spurgeon, Moody, each shared a common denominator: a fire in their belly. They each were so eaten up with the Gospel and thirsty for Christ and filled with the Holy Ghost—they could not stand idly by while others perished. They saw nothing but eternity, worshipped a Holy God, and served a Risen Christ; living not for earth nor its gains but living only for heaven and its rewards. When they preached, they linked the Devil with sin and the Cross with salvation. They preached Hell and its fire and Christ and Him crucified. Not one of the feared King, Queen, or Pope; and not one of them sought the compliments of men."

E. A. Johnston

WE NEED TIMES LIKE THESE

"In 1740 when God moved through New England it was called 'The Great Awakening.' Revival has often been referred to as 'an awakening.' At Gethsemane Jesus faced the 'crises point' of His earthly ministry and His disciples slept right through it. Today the church is in a 'crises point' and we are sleeping right through it."

E. A. Johnston

"There is a golden thread that weaves its way through revivals and if this purified thread is broken it has been a bar to revivals throughout history. To which I refer is the golden thread a forgiving heart toward others. When one researches the history of revival it is plainly shown that some revivals began accompanied by a sudden manifestation of God's presence, when Christians began to confess their sins of pride or an unforgiving heart to one another."

E. A. Johnston

"The year 1886 was memorable for five significant events. A fatal riot (February 6-9, in Seattle, Washington); A devastating hurricane (August 20, in Indianola, Texas); A ground shaking earthquake (August 31, in Charleston, South Carolina); A formal dedication (October 28, New York Harbor, Statue of Liberty). Did I mention the last? Oh, yes, Sam Jones came to town."

E. A. Johnston

"John Wesley and George Whitefield stood out like two brilliant diamonds against the dark velvet background of a degenerate Age and an apostate church, mainly comprised of an unconverted ministry."

E. A. Johnston

"Jonathan Edwards knew the glory of revival and the cost of revival. After seeing God move in several seasons of glorious revival, the last fourteen years of Edward's life were filled with trouble, trial, grief, opposition, turmoil, termination, and hardship. He had to witness the early death of his young friend, David Brainerd, who died in Edward's home in Northhampton, MA, at the age of 29. Four months later he suffered the personal loss of the sudden death of his eighteen-year-old darling, daughter Jerusha (who lies buried beside Brainerd in Bridge Street Cemetery). He was then thrust into a scene of great controversy and opposition in his own church which resulted in his removal. He and his large family were suddenly thrust into privation and cast upon the world without any financial support and Edwards and his family ended up in the wilderness of Stockbridge, MA, with a ministry of preaching to a mere handful of Indians. While laboring there in inclement weather he came down with a severe fever that made him an invalid for a period of seven months, which greatly weakened his already strained constitution. From there he had a brief promotion to the Presidency of the College of New Jersey, only to die before assuming his labors at the age of 54 from a fatal reaction to a new vaccine. He died with the weight of the world upon him as he entered a better world, where pain, suffering, and struggle were no more. By the way, did I mention that these last fourteen years of Jonathan Edward's life were his greatest period of productivity? It was during that time he wrote the bulk of his written legacy to the Church at large."

E. A. Johnston

"He was called 'The Wonder of the Ages' and 'The Sledgehammer'. Listening to Sam Jones preach was both an enjoyable and painful experience. Enjoyable because he got you to laugh about yourself and others; painful because his sledgehammer preaching unearthed all the vermin hidden for years beneath a false foundation of self-righteousness and fabricated veneer of self-delusion."

E. A. Johnston

"Visiting the scenes of revival by tracing the steps of men whom God has used in former times, is an unforgettable experience that will last a lifetime. To stand where Whitefield stood, Wesley stood, Edwards stood, Finney stood, Moody and Jones stood, and to allow one's mind to replay the very scenes that transpired there and transformed lives those many years ago, is both invigorating to the soul and challenging to the heart to go out and do likewise in your day and mine."

E. A. Johnston

THE COST OF REVIVAL

"Anyone who begins to preach for revival will soon face fierce opposition from lost religious men. For when the great doctrines of the Ruin, Redemption, Repentance, and Regeneration are faithfully proclaimed then all hell will break loose. I've had deacons face me down in the sanctuary with fire in their eyes because I said, 'Unless you repent you will surely bust Hell wide open when you die.'"

E. A. Johnston

"There is a great deal of insincerity concerning revival among the people of God. Many will quote Second Chronicles 7:14 which states, 'If my people, which are called by my name, shall humble themselves, and pray, and seek my face, and turn from their wicked ways; then will I hear from heaven, and will forgive their sin, and will heal their land.' Very few indeed, however, are willing to comply with ALL the demands of God in this verse. There are those who are willing to humble themselves and seek God in prayer for revival, but Hell will freeze over before they ever part with their pet sins or leave their wicked ways. They are like the man who sincerely desires a deeper walk with God and who is willing to even engage in agonizing prayer at their own personal Gethsemane—but it stops there. They fail to go on to Calvary where a Cross awaits, ready to be embraced in a painful, self-exposed crucifixion."

E. A. Johnston

"Revival is not only possible, it is probable, so long as we are expendable."

E. A. Johnston

WHY WE NEED REVIVAL IN OUR DAY

"We must be careful when labeling heightened religious activity as revival. Just because there is a sense of the supernatural in worship, religious emotional experience, and growing attendance, does not necessarily denominate a true revival of religion. False fire is the work Satan from a false spirit that misleads many who are ignorant of how God has moved in former times in real periods of revival and spiritual awakening. There is a lot of nonsense that has been called 'revival' when God had nothing at all to do with it at all."

E. A. Johnston

"When Jesus was here in His earthly ministry, as He passed through towns and villages, those who encountered Him experienced change. Revival is an encounter with Christ Jesus. The Apostle John encountered the Risen Christ on the Isle of Patmos and he fell down as one dead. Revival is a vital encounter with a Living Lord to where you are dead to sin, dead to self, dead to reputation, and dead to the world. The first concern of those in the midst revival is their own sinfulness before a holy God as they are confronted with the glory of God; then there is humility and sincere repentance and a turning from sin; then there is a desire for the pursuit of holiness and continual corporate prayer; this all rises in passion for a concern and burden for the lost and perishing which results in active vital evangelism."

E. A. Johnston

HINDRANCES TO REVIVAL

"Why are the Christians in the Book of Acts turning the world upside down? Why aren't we turning the world upside down in our day? Because the dissimilarities are obvious enough to shame us."

E. A. Johnston

"Our only hope today is revival and reformation in our pulpits across the land. We must cease the madness of continuing with a man-centered gospel that is centered around the happiness of man; and we must return to the God-centered gospel that was prominent during times of historical revival and spiritual awakening and proclaim that man is a sinner, God is holy, and there is a future Judgment for all mankind. That man is not only ruined by Adam's fall, he is a rebel at heart because of his natural condition which is enmity toward God. And man has a poison in the blood where the only remedy is the shed Blood of Christ for pardon of sin. And that God is the author of salvation and not man. That being a Christian means being born from above and washed in the Blood and we must point sinners once again to a bloody Cross where a bloodstained Savior bore the sin of many so we can live."

E. A. Johnston

A WARNING TO PREACHERS

"The Book of Ezekiel contains the following warning to both sinner and preacher: 'When I say unto the wicked, Thou shalt surely die; and thou givest him not warning, nor speakest to warn the wicked from his wicked way, to save his life; the same wicked man shall die in his inquity; but his blood will I require at thine hand.' At the Last Judgment we will be able to recognize the preachers who were into self-preservation and self-promotion—they will be the ones standing there with BLOODY HANDS."

E. A. Johnston

BEING JEALOUS FOR GOD

"If the Church will not defend His holy Name then the Almighty must. God will either pour out His blessings in revival to defend His holy Name, or He will pour out His wrath upon mankind to avenge His holy Name. It will either be a defending or avenging to show forth His glory and to remind mankind He alone is the Sovereign ruler of all."

E. A. Johnston

GOING DEEPER WITH GOD

"God gets serious with those who get serious with Him."

E. A. Johnston

"God's Word is true and God is true to His Word."

E. A. Johnston

"God is a Dynamite God who does super-duper things. Do you believe that?"

E. A. Johnston

"I may have failed Jesus from time to time but He has NEVER failed me once."

E. A. Johnston

COLLECTION FIVE:

HOT COALS FOR THE ALTAR OF YOUR HEART

"You are either out & out for God or on the outs with God."

E. A. Johnston

"If you find yourself like one of the Christians in the Laodecian church in a lukewarm state in regard to your walk with God, then you need to do either of the following: stick your head in a bucket of ice water until you wake up; or go sit on some hot coals until you catch fire and jump up. But you need to do something or you'll just rot and be good for nothing."

E. A. Johnston

"God can't use anyone who is neutral—but God can use anyone who is combustible."

E. A. Johnston

"Jesus said, 'Take up your cross and follow me.' He didn't say, 'Go your own way and I will follow you.'"

E. A. Johnston

"Brother Pastor, Jesus is not impressed that you run 3,000 on Sunday. Most of the time He ran 12."

E. A. Johnston

"The Devil had his cards stacked up against me: I grew up in a godless home that was haunted. My father was an agnostic and my grandfather was a mob boss. Then a pastor across the alley by the name of Clem Dear got a burden on his heart for my soul—this man wouldn't let me go to Hell. He prayed the first prayer for me I ever heard drop from a person's lips; he gave me my first job in his bible book store; he gave me my first bible; he was instrumental in my being part of a revival meeting where the Canadian evangelist Ernest W. Wakefield preached the gospel of the Cross to me. I got saved that night as a thirteen year old boy. And 56 years later, as an old man, a Sovereign God dropped the recording of that evening from December 1968 into my lap and I listened once more to the preaching of the gospel that saved me. I heard myself sing as a thirteen year old boy the hymns we sang that remarkable evening; on that recording I heard myself cough as I had a chronic asthmatic cough as a teenager. My God is a dynamite God who does super duper things! He can secretly record an event in past times and 56 years later hand you that recording just to prove He is a sovereign ruler over "all things."

E. A. Johnston

"Jesus told His disciples to "tarry in the city until you are endued with power from on high" (Luke 24:49). But we today misunderstood Him to say, "go out into the city unendued and without power."

E. A. Johnston

"Jesus didn't build institutions to be occupied. Rather, He built individuals to go out and occupy."

E. A. Johnston

"Sin is the blackest, darkest, vilest, filthiest, staining thing in the world. But God's Word declares: 'Come now, and let us reason together saith the LORD: though your sins be as scarlet, they shall be as white as snow; though they be red like crimson, they shall be as wool" (Isaiah 1:18). Have you washed your sins in the laundry of Christ's Blood?"

E. A. Johnston

JOLTS FROM JOHNSTON

"If God is a dynamite God who does super duper things, then how come you've been acting like a dud?"

E. A. Johnston

"God is looking for the individual who is willing to lose it all so Christ can be their all-in-all."

E. A. Johnston

"If you are a pastor who does not preach repentance then there is a good chance that you haven't repented yourself."

E. A. Johnston

"The church that is into self-preservation is an institution full of itself with no room for the Christ who sacrificed Himself."

E. A. Johnston

"I visited a church that looked like a nightclub, the pastor told embarrassing bathroom jokes before he prayed; his message was just funny stories about his family, and the rock music was so loud it hurt my ears. When I left I felt sorry for the spiritually drunken members of that nightclub that passed itself off as a church led by a nightclub entertainer."

E. A. Johnston

"If holiness is not something you pursue then worldliness is something you enjoy."

E. A. Johnston

"If you're on your coach watching TV more than you are in your Bible and on your face in prayer, then don't be surprised if your family goes to hell around you."

E. A. Johnston

"An empty religious profession means you are a church member in good standing who is sitting on a rotten foundation of self-righteousness, self-reliance, and self-satisfaction."

E. A. Johnston

"Unless you repent you will surely bust Hell wide open when you die—even if you are the Chairman of the deacons."

E. A. Johnston

"If you think you are good enough for Heaven because you are not bad enough for Hell then it is probable that you have never been born from above and washed in the Blood."

E. A. Johnston

"Vital Christianity means you are empty of self and full of the Holy Ghost."

E. A. Johnston

"You're either all out for God or you're not. God will never honor a divided heart."

E. A. Johnston

"Christ held nothing back at Calvary. He won't accept anything less than our absolute surrender."

E. A. Johnston

"Revival is something we need when we are not right. And when we are not right we need revival."

E. A. Johnston

"Years ago, I woke up in the middle of the night and I thought I was having a heart attack. I had been working fourteen hour days and getting up at 4:30am each morning to have my quiet time. I was plumb worn out. I was carrying on a full time ministry and a full time secular career as a stockbroker. And as I sat there at 2am at my desk before my open Bible, I asked the Lord to come get me and take me home—I was so exhausted I just wanted Heaven. I told Him: "I'm ready to come home Lord. Will you come get me?" And He met me there in those early morning hours by speaking to my heart—not an audible voice but a Voice nonetheless. In the Gospels Jesus usually answered a question with a question. That morning he answered my question with a question: "What do you do for a living?" I answered, "Investments". He said, "I have an investment in you and I will receive the dividends from my investment." Case closed. I went back to bed. That was 18 years ago—there have been a lot of dividends paid during that time."

E. A. Johnston

"I was at the grocery store getting ready to check out my groceries when a pushy woman jumped in front of me and cut in line ahead of me. Looking at her I knew I had seen her before but where? Her face was so familiar to me—then it hit me. She was the featured solo singer in the church choir last Sunday."

E. A. Johnston

"When you booze you lose. Do you booze?"

E. A. Johnston

JACOB'S WRESTLINGS

"It was said of Jacob that he was so crooked he could hide behind a corkscrew! God straightened Jacob out at Jabbok in the shadow of Esau coming with 400 men. Have we faced a crises of our own 'Personal Jabbok'? Have we been straightened out?"

E. A. Johnston

Jacob left Jabbok with a limp from wrestling with God, but he learned to lean on God the rest of his life. After the wrestling, Jacob had to use a cane for with every step he winced in pain—and with every step the self- life died a little more."

E. A. Johnston

"Jacob may have been saved at Bethel but he was conquered at Peniel."

E. A. Johnston

"Jacob finished his up and down life in Egypt, emerging at the very last upon the plane of triumphant faith and prophecy."

E. A. Johnston

LIFE IS SHORT

"We're all gonna die sooner or later. If you go all out for Christ and the Gospel you may run a shorter course like a Stephen or a Brainerd; or you may run long like Abraham or a Moses. But either way, all that really matters is not how long or short your service to God was but how well."

E. A. Johnston

"The day after my daughter graduated college I had a heart attack. All four of my main arteries were 90% (ninety percent) blocked—I should have died. I was in the hospital for over two months and went through a quadruple bypass surgery and I now wear a pacemaker and a defibrillator. We can leave this world any minute quite suddenly and unexpectedly. Are we living in light of eternity? Are we advancing the kingdom of God in our lifetime? Do we witness to the lost and perishing? Or are we merely consumed with the world and occupied with the things of the world? Or are we intoxicated with Christ and on fire for God? We could leave this world quite unexpectedly and suddenly."

E. A. Johnston

C. T. Studd's little poem should challenge us all to live more for eternity.

"Only one life, 'twill soon be past;

Only what's done for Christ will last

AMERICA
REVIVAL OR RUIN?

Bible Text: Amos, Chapter Four.
Preached on: Wednesday July 25, 2012.

Comments Sent to Dr. Johnston

(11/12/2024)

"Self Examination"

This sermon brought out some important points that we as Christians should adhere to. Especially 2 Chronicles 7:14, which is our pathway to revival not just as individuals but as a nation.

(4/7/2022)

"Great Sermon!"

Child of God from Florida

Thank you. God's greatest blessings to you.

(1/26/2022)

"Very Appropriate Message"

Josey Wales from Dixieland

A very convicting message in this day of reprobation. God's wrath will surely fall on this wicked, rebellious nation.

(1/25/2022)

"Great Sermon!"

Arthur Churms from South Africa

Thank you so much Revd Johnston for giving us such a down to earth sermon—pulling no punches. It is utterly refreshing to hear straight preaching. Every blessing to you and your congregation. Arthur

(8/22/2021)

"Great Sermon!"

Dan Conseen from Cherokee, NC

What a blessing and encouragement to know men still stand in boldness crying out against sin.

(5/30/2020)

"Great Sermon!"

From Stephanie

This is the type of sermon we all need to hear especially right now. I am so thankful there are pastors out there who can actually preach like this. Praise God. This is definitely a sermon to be shared, and a call to repent which is the only hope for our nation.

(10/25/2019)

"Great Sermon!"

Thankful to God from Florida

This man TRULY loves the Lord. I have been searching for no less than five years for a pastor who would truly preach the TRUE words of God from a real bible rather from perverted bible knock-offs. It it were not for SermonAudio and a few other Christian sites, I would never hear the kind of preaching such as Brother E. A. Johnston and others. I open this site several times every day (and night)...Thank you Lord for supplying my great need and desire for Your truths made available to me through SermonAudio.

(10/27/2018)

"A Message for American Christians!"

Yolanda from AZ

Choose ye this day who you will serve.

(11/18/2018)

"THANK YOU"

Timothy from WASHINGTON STATE

Very powerful. We all need to come back to our Loving GOD. Before it is too late.

(4/24/2016)

"Great Sermon!"

Mark M from UK

A powerful convicting message. The Church in England is sleeping too. The nation that once, under God, gave the English speaking world the King James Bible and exported missionaries around the globe, now exports the profanation of marriage and other evils. May it please the Lord to wake us before His judgment falls. Thank you for this message Dr. Johnston. May God have mercy upon us.

(4/26/2015)

"Great Sermon!"

Rita Lim from Singapore

Excellent message. Succinct and direct. Thank you for this message!

(3/12/2015)

"Great Sermon!"

Geoff Bishop from Australia

I am sad to say that the condition of America is the same as here in Australia. I truly believe judgment is approaching, people need to flee to Jesus.

(8/12/2014)

"Great Sermon!"

Brenda Miller from Charlotte, NC

So true. LORD bring the nation to repentance and cause the ministers that are not preaching the Word of God to repent. People are dying everyday and going to hell.

(7/8/2014)

"Great Sermon!"

Ross Hankins from Indiana

Great message. It took me back to the 50's when things were as he said and made me long for those days. I'm sure Israel experience those same longings when they departed from the Lord. Pray His will is to restore our nation or hasten His return.

(12/18/2013)

"How Many Have Ears to Hear the Call?"

Mrs. Lori Jackson from Oakland, Maine

This is not just a call from a man surrendered to the Lord, but it is an urgent call from the Spirit of the Living God to those who profess to follow Christ. Search our hearts, Oh God...see if there be any wicked ways in me that I may turn from them and repent for my sins. May the Lord hear our prayers and send His mighty revival upon us, our families, and our nation. Time is short!

(6/30/2013)

"Strong Sermon!"

Floridahank from Deerfield Beach, Florida

Bro. Johnston brings out good questions for the church as to what we're willing to do to change the course of our country. Time is running out and God's judgements are already being felt by our country. The question is will we repent and ask God for forgiveness or will things just get worse because of our sins.

(10/21/2012)

"Great Sermon!"

Amy from Georgia

Amen!

(10/5/2012)

"Great Sermon!"

Kim from West Virginia

A message from God's Heart to our ears. This should be preached from every pulpit. God Bless you Pastor for your obedience.

(9/21/2012)

"Amen!"

Kevin from Wyoming USA

This Brother is telling it straight as an arrow. We have turned our back on the grace of God in our foolish pride.

(9/20/2012)

"Getting serious with GOD!"

Rebecca from Singapore

A sermon I need to hear...A sermon to be preached from every pulpit...A sermon that caused me to examine myself and reconsider my walk with GOD. For CHRIST alone is worthy!

(9/17/2012)

"Superb Sermon!"

Samantha M from Georgia Camden County

Praise God for this message...God Bless you Pastor Johnston!

(7/25/2012)

"Great Sermon!"

Janine from Louisiana

We need revival Lord. Another Great Awakening...we need revival Lord, and let it start with me.

(7/25/2012)

"Powerful plea"

Brother GG from Abbotsford, BC, Canada

So few men of God are giving true warnings from the heart of God for the church in America. Never before is there a need for trumpet blast wake up calls to the church that are needed. E. A. Johnston gives us a clear sound from the burden of the Lord he carries. May the church be roused to repentance and prayer. A practical response would be to have a weekly prayer meeting in your church for revival.

AMERICA: REVIVAL OR RUIN MESSAGE?

When I was a little boy in the 1950's, things were different back then. I remember this country when Hollywood had censors, politicians had a conscience, and America had a moral compass. Hemlines were lower and moral were higher and sin was called sin and not social disorders. Of course, we didn't have the technology that we have today. Back then if you said Microsoft they thought you were referring to your mattress. And we didn't have Wi-Fi. We had hi-fi. It was a time when only sailors had tattoos.

I remember America when it still had a strong work ethic and business abounded in honesty and integrity and a man's word and handshake were as good as gold. And I remember an America when a parent did not have to worry about what their children saw on TV and marriage was between a man and a woman. There was such a thing as shame in society back then.

I remember America when the church still had authority and there was still a fear of God in the land. I remember a nation that stood on biblical principles and looked to God for guidance and to the church for direction. It was okay to pray in public school back then and the Ten Commandments were publicly displayed. And if any atheist cried out against it, there were more than enough Christians to shout that person down because God had the majority in the nation back then. And I remember an America that was looked up to by other nations and we were a country that held on to the principles of our founding fathers and Old Glory was never stomped on and set on fire because we respected too much what it stood for.

Back then there was such a thing as a weekly prayer meeting in the church and people actually came to pray. And they weren't embarrassed to cry when they prayed and they prayed loud and long and did so until they grabbed hold of God and the fire fell and consumed the sacrifice. The church back then didn't operate on money and manpower, but by prayer and Holy Ghost power. Back then the church influenced society instead of society influencing the church. And I remember preachers who preached about the Blood and the Cross and they warned that Hell was hot and a future Judgment awaited all mankind. Those kind of preachers weren't afraid of men, but they sure feared the Almighty.

I keep using the word "remember" because all I have is my memory of these former things. Today America is facing ruin and only a heaven-sent revival will save this nation from complete destruction.

You see Christianity was always meant to be counter-cultural. In the New Testament, when the church met the world, there was a clash because the church went in one direction and pagan society went in the other. Now they travel side by side and there is just a rub between them.

We wanted to reach the world so we brought the world into the church. Where has that gotten us? It has only corrupted the house of God. When the people of God begin to drift away from the heart of God, then God will send remedial judgments to call His people back to Him.

My message today is entitled, "America: Revival or Ruin. " It is about the remedial judgments of God and we want to begin in the Book of Amos, chapters 3 and 4.

Amos was a fiery prophet of God whose main message was judgment. God's timetable was up and the people of God would not return to Him, so He sent a series of judgments upon them; remedial judgments, each one being stronger and harsher than the previous one. God was seeking to get their attention, but they refused to listen. Is God seeking to get our attention today? Is America under the chastisement of the Almighty? Have we not turned our backs on God in this country today?

You know, 9/11 was a wake-up call, but almost everyone went back to sleep. God is still in His mercy, seeking to get our attention. But the timetable is quickly running out. This is the most critical time in the history of this nation, because if things don't drastically change and there is a turning of this nation back to God, then there will be no nation to turn. It will be gone!

Look at ancient Rome and their military might that ruled the world with an iron fist. Can you fear an Italian army today? No. it is laughable. America is now laughable in the eyes of the world.

Well, look in your Bibles at Amos chapter 3, verse 3. What does it say? "Can two walk together, except they be agreed?" Can you walk with God and still hang on to your wretched sins? Can you name the name of Christ and live like the devil? If you want to walk with God you must turn from your sins and pursue a life of holiness. God is holy. God's Word declares, "Follow...holiness without which no man shall see the Lord" (Hebrews 12:14).

The problem with Israel here in Amos was that they had quit walking with God. They preferred their sins over God. And yet they still believed they were all right in God's eyes; that God had somehow adjusted Himself to their wicked ways; that He tolerated their sins because of His great love for them. God was angry with the Jews and God is angry with the church member who claims to be a Christian yet who still hangs onto his sins.

"Can two walk together, except they be agreed?" Can they?

Picture in your mind the story of Elijah and his contest with the prophets of Baal on Mount Carmel. He was up against 450 prophets of Baal; remember that? Elijah built an altar and challenged the prophets of Baal to call on their gods to consume the sacrifice and their gods didn't show up. Finally, Elijah began to mock them and said that perhaps their god was on vacation. But listen to what Elijah said to the assembled crowd that day. "And Elijah came unto all the people, and said, How long halt ye between two opinions? If the LORD be God, follow Him, but if Baal, then follow him. And the people answered him not a word" (1 Kings 18:21).

In other words, if you want to walk with God, you can't have one foot with God and with the other play footsie with the world. Notice he said, "if the LORD be God." Is Jesus your Lord? Or is He just your insurance policy against hell?

In Amos chapter 3, verse 6 the text reads: "shall there be evil (calamity) in a city, and the LORD hath not done it?"

Never in my lifetime have there been so many frequent natural disasters in this country, one right after another. What do you think that is? Is it global warming or mother nature? Or is it God allowing Satan to wreak havoc on our society and on our land? In the Book of Job, Satan brought a great wind to collapse the house of Job and remove his family and his wealth. God gave Satan permission to do it. Satan is not on the same level as God. There is not an equal war between good and evil. Satan is only a created being; a judged created being whose time is short and he knows it. The Last Days will be so terrible you will not want to be alive if God does not send revival.

Let us now look at how God sends remedial judgments to a people who have turned their backs on Him. Look at Amos chapter 4 beginning in verse 6: "And I also have given you cleanness of teeth in all your cities, and want of bread in all your places; yet have ye not returned unto me, saith the LORD."

Judgment Number One was that God sent a famine in the land. In His mercy, He sent them a famine. But how did they respond? "Yet have ye not returned unto me, saith the LORD."

Well, look at Judgment Number Two in verse 7. It is more severe. "And also, I have withholden the rain from you, when there were yet three months to the harvest: and I caused it to rain upon one city, and caused it not to rain upon another city: one piece was rained upon, and the piece whereupon it rained not withered."

See, you can go a week without food, but man cannot live long without water. God sent a drought to His disobedient people. Now do they turn back to Him and repent and seek His face?

No. "...yet have ye not returned unto me, saith the LORD."

You see, back than the local Jewish weatherman told them it was just mother nature acting up again. They would just have to grin and bear it. But they didn't return to God. So He brings an even more severe judgment. Look at Judgment Number Three in verse 9: "I have smitten you with blasting and mildew, when your gardens and your vineyards and your fig trees and your olive trees increased, the palmerworm devoured them: yet have ye not returned unto me, saith the LORD."

God sent a financial collapse. Our economy is growing worse and worse and a global depression is on the horizon. Have we turned back to God? God is seeking to get our attention. Are we paying attention or are we asleep? The remedial judgments of God when unheeded become the increasing judgments of God.

Look at how severe Judgment Number Four is. Look at verse 10: "I have sent among you the pestilence after the manner of Egypt; your young men have I slain with the sword, and have taken away your horses; and I have made the stink of your camps to come up unto your nostrils; yet have ye not returned unto me, saith the LORD."

He has removed the young men of the city by death. You know, take the young men out of a community and the community has little future. God sent death to them through pestilence and war. What is it going to take in America? What kind of terrible national calamity will have to fall upon this nation before it turns back to God? Will it ever turn back to God? When the Christian leaders refuse to acknowledge that God is judging America and judging the churches in America, then we have the blind leading the blind.

Pastors of former generations were wiser and preached revival sermons to turn the hearts of the people back to God. Listen to a sermon preached by a leading pastor in Boston in 1755 when an earthquake shook that city. Listen to the title of his sermon:

"Earthquakes the works of God and tokens of his just displeasure being a discourse on that subject wherein a particular description of this awful event of Providence made public at this time on occasion of the late dreadful earthquake which happened on the 18th of November 1755."

The text of the sermon was Psalm 18:7: "Then the earth shook and trembled; the foundations also of the hills moved and were shaken, because he was wroth."

The leading pastors in New England all preached similar sermons at that time. They called their congregations to fast and pray and repent of their sins and fall on their faces before the God of terrible majesty! Even the President of the United States had a fear of God back then and called the entire nation to a time of humiliation before an offended Creator. Consider this notice in a newspaper from 1798. "A discourse delivered in the First Presbyterian Church of Philadelphia on Wednesday, May 9, 1798, recommended by the President of the United States to be observed as a day of fasting, humiliation and prayer throughout the United States of America."

How much more urgent is the great need for America today? We can't look to the White House to help us. We can't even look to the church house to help us. Who will take a stand for God in this land today? Who? It is time for the people of God to turn from their wicked ways and fast and pray and seek His holy face in repentance and humiliation or there will not be a nation left to pray in! When will the churches in the land stop "playing church" and get right with God and call a time of solemn assembly, where the people of God cry out to God in nights of desperation and prayer? Why complain about the direction of this nation when you are not willing to do anything about it? God says, "Return to me, and I will return unto you" (Malachi 3:7).

How bad do we want Him? listen to this warning from the Book of Romans:

"The night is far spent, the day is at hand: let us therefore cast off the works of darkness, and let us put on the amour of light. Let us walk honestly, as in the day: not in rioting and drunkenness, not in chambering and wantonness, not in strife and envying. But put ye on the Lord Jesus Christ, and make not provision for the flesh, to fulfill the lusts thereof" (Romans 13:12-14).

Let me tell you what can happen to a church. Things can get between you and God. Leonard Ravenhill used to tell a story about a friend of his who was on fire for God. Every time Ravenhill got around this man, he was more thirsty for Christ and things of eternal worth. Do you know people like that? People that make you thirsty for God? Well, this man was like that. Every time he got around him all he wanted to talk about was Jesus and winning souls. Then one day he began collecting stamps. As his collection grew, so did his enthusiasm for stamp collecting. Leonard Ravenhill said, "This man called me up one day and said, 'Come on over and I will show you my new stamp collection of British Colonials that cost me $50,000.'" Ravenhill said that pretty soon this man no longer wanted to talk about Jesus or the things of God. He just wanted to talk about stamps. Imagine. A harmless "little thing" like a stamp drew that man away from God.

What is it with you? What is the thing in your life friend, no matter how seemingly harmless, that has stolen your affection from Jesus? Why is your Bible a closed book? Why is your prayer life so stale and so infrequent? Why is your walk with God so up and down?

You see, a church has influence for God in a community as long as the church members have influence with God. A church is only a reflection of its members. The members of a church will either draw people to God like a magnet or turn people away from Him by their inconsistent and worldly lives.

Let me share a story with you. A traveling preacher was passing through a certain city, and he wanted to go by and visit a historic church that had a long reputation for doing good for the Lord. But when he got into town, he stopped at a local restaurant to grab some lunch and ask directions to that famous church. The owner of the restaurant was well familiar with that church and when the traveling preacher went on and on about all the great things that church had done, the owner of the restaurant looked at him strangely, and commented: "Yes, it used to be that way some time ago. If you want directions to that church go up the road a piece and turn right at the next stop sign. Then go up a hill and at the top of the hill there will be a sign telling you the way to that church." "What does the sign say?" asked the traveling preacher. The man paused, and with a sad look said, "The sign says, CAUTION: CHILDREN AT PLAY."

I am sorry to say I have known churches like that. Too many. Churches that once did great things for God, that God did great things through them, but now there are signs out front that say, CAUTION: CHILDREN AT PLAY.

The hour is late friends. It is time to get serious with God. Get serious with God and God will get serious with you. If your free time is spent on anything other than prayer and Bible study and things of eternal worth—I feel sorry for you! There is a Bema Seat for believers, and it is there we will receive gold, silver, and precious stones or wood, hay, and straw. When the works of your life pass through the fire what will remain? Will it be gold, silver, and precious stones? Will your life for Christ shine like a brilliant jewel reflecting His glory? Or will you stand there knee deep in the ashes of a wasted life and bend over to scoop up those ashes and press those ashes into His nail-pierced Hands? Do you want to be found playing with the marbles of the world when Jesus appears at the rapture? If we really believe we are living in the Last Days, our lives don't reflect it. If we really believed that Christ is returning soon, we would not be so consumed with this world. Some of you within the sound of my voice may be living your last years. How do you want to spend them? Chasing a little white ball around a golf course? I used to do that until God showed me what golf stood for—Golden Opportunities Lost Forever!

What occupies your time? Are we redeeming the time because the days are evil? You may think I am morbid, but I read the obituaries every day. I take time to read each one and contemplate on their life and how they lived it. "He was an avid golfer. He loved to ride motorcycles. He had a passion for bowling and he was a deacon at such and such Baptist church."

Seldom do I read an obituary about a man that says: "He had a passion for God and was consumed with things of eternal worth. He lived to bring the lost in. He loved Jesus with his whole heart." No. It is usually, "He loved his antique cars, or his bass boat, and so on." I read a obituary recently about a church member whose friend wrote the article an she said the deceased loved martinis!

Like I said, you can learn a lot about a person by what consumes their time here on earth. My late mentor, Dr. Stephen F. Olford, used to quote:

"Only one life, 'twill soon be past;
Only what's done for Christ will last."

But, I repeat, only a heaven-sent revival will save America from ruin. These are indeed the End Times. Do you believe that? And the end is drawing closer and closer every day. We are living in the day of the spirit of Antichrist right now. Our society grows darker and darker with each new day. You'd better forget about your theory of "relax and be raptured". I believe in the Rapture of the Church, but I believe the American church is going through fire and persecution before Christ comes again. Persecution is on the way to America—and it is right around the corner. The chaff will be separated from the wheat.

But there is hope of revival for America. The Word of God gives us a pathway to revival. It is found in 2 Chronicles, chapter 7 and verse 14:

"If my people, which are called by my name, shall humble themselves, and pray, and seek my face, and turn from their wicked ways; then will I hear from heaven, and will forgive their sin, and will heal their land."

Let me ask you a question. Does our land need healing? Let me ask you the next question. Are you willing to pay the price for revival and really do what this verse says and get serious with God and humble yourself before Him? Will you pray and seek His face in these dark days? And are you willing to do the last part of this verse which God requires from us? And that is to turn from your wicked ways? Are you willing to repent of your sins and come clean with God? Not only for your sake and the sake of your family, but for the sake of our nation? For the nation is merely the reflection of its people. America used to be a God-fearing nation because the Christians used to fear God and live holy lives toward Him. We are to be salt, the Bible says. You see, salt is a preservative. We are to be a preservative from evil for this nation to do good for the glory of God.

Listen friends: God promises us in His Word, "Return unto me, and I will return unto you" (Malachi 3:7). Are we willing to do it with a sincere heart? The passage in Second Chronicles mentions duties on our part that we must do to gain the ear of the Almighty. I believe the average church member is willing to do the first two aspects of this text: humble themselves and pray. But very few are willing to comply with the most solemn aspect of this text, and that is repent and turn from their wicked ways.

Listen to me. God will not move one skinny inch until we comply with His demands of repentance on our part. If we humbly seek His face in prayer and supplication and turn from our wicked ways, He then promises to do two BIG THINGS for us: hear and heal. This is an if/then proposition in Scripture. IF the people of God will do such and such, THEN God will do such and such. God says that if my people do these things, then will I hear their prayers and heal their land.

You see, there was a revival in the days of Hezekiah, because he complied with the precepts of 2 Chronicles 7:14. King Hezekiah gathered his religious leaders together and told them, "Hear me, ye Levites, sanctify now yourselves, and sanctify the house of the LORD God of your fathers, and carry forth the filthiness out of the holy place" (2 Chronicles 29:5).

Hezekiah was instructing them to do two things. Number One: clean the temple of its idols and Number Two: clean the altar of their hearts in repentance. We see this in 2 Chronicles chapter 29 and verses 15-16. Listen to what the people of God did in response to the king's request of getting right with God. The text reads:

"And they gathered their brethren, and sanctified themselves, and came, according to the commandment of the king, by the words of the LORD, to cleanse the house of the LORD. And the priests went into the inner part of the house of the LORD, to cleanse it, and brought out all the uncleanness that they found in the temple of the LORD into the court of the house of the LORD. And the Levites took it, to carry it out abroad into the brook Kidron."

This is what the people of God did. They searched the temple to find unclean idols and then brought them out, took them to the brook Kidron, and BURNED them there, they sanctified themselves and God brought a mighty revival under King Hezekiah because he did that which was right in the sight of the Lord.

It is up to the Church in America today to do the same. To search our sanctuaries to see what idols we have set up which displease and grieve God and take these worldly idols back out of our churches and GET RID OF THEM. Then we are to search our hearts under the bright spotlight of the Holy Spirit to see if there is anything grievous to God in our lives and then we must TURN FROM IT IN REPENTANCE. Then, and only then, will our prayers have power with God to the degree that He will indeed HEAR and HEAL: HEAR our prayers and HEAL our land.

You know, we don't hear much preaching today on the cross in the life of the believer. But if we want God to hear us and to take us seriously, we must crucify anything in our lives that is displeasing to

Christ Jesus! When we get serious with God, He will get serious with us and answer our prayers and bring a Holy Ghost revival to America that will shake the gates of hell from coast to coast!

This is a call to fall on our faces and seek Him in sincerity of heart. Will we do it? Will we do it? America: Revival or Ruin? Will we heed the warnings? God help us if we don't!

ABOUT THE AUTHOR

E.A. Johnston in the Outdoor pulpit at Hanham Mount where George Whitefield preached, courtesy of Digby James.

E. A. Johnston, Ph.D., D. B. S., is a Fellow with the Stephen Olford Institute for Biblical Preaching and is an evangelist and author with twenty eight published books. He is the founder of Evangelism Awakening, a revival-based ministry whose focus is the study of historical revival and preaching for revival in our day. He has over two thousand sermons on SermonAudio.com.

FOUR PHOTOS

Author at D.L. Moody's Gravestone at
Round Top, Northfield, MA

Author at David Brainerd's Grave
Marker at
Bridge Street Cemetery,
Northhampton, MA

Author at Asahel Nettleton Grave
Marker at
East Windser, CT

Author at the spot of George Whitefield's Last Open-Air Sermon Where He Preached to 4,000, Exeter, NH and Died the Next Morning

SOME OF THE BOOKS BY E. A. JOHNSTON

Many of the following books may be purchased individually or as a set by going to Dr. Johnston's webpage in the bookstore at The Old Paths Publications that has links to distributors. Go to:

www.theoldpathspublications.com/Pages/Authors/Johnston.htm

or

Email us:
TOP@theoldpathspublications.com

1. "A Heart Awake: The Authorized Biography of J. Sidlow Baxter" Foreword by Adrian Rogers (The Old Paths Publications, www.theoldpathspublications.com).

2. "Realities Of Revival" Foreword by Stephen F. Olford (Gospel Folio Press, Canada; 2005).

3. "No Turning Back" (Gospel Folio Press, Canada; 2005).

4. "The Master's Plan: Unfolding God's Blueprint For Your Life" (Gospel Folio Press, Canada; 2006).

5. "Know The Book: Bible Survey At A Glance" (Gospel Folio Press, Canada; 2007).

6. "Jua Kitabu: Tazamo la Biblia" Know The Book translated into the Swahili by missionary G. I. Harlow (Everyday Publications, Canada; 2007).

7. "Walking With God" Foreword by Ted S. Rendall (Gospel Folio Press, Canada; 2007).

8. "Return To Me: Entering A Right Relationship With God" (Gospel Folio Press, Canada; 2007).

9. "Are You In The Book Of Life?" (Gospel Folio Press, Canada; 2008).

10. "Call To Revival" Foreword By Colin Peckham (Gospel Folio Press, Canada; 2008).

11. "The Church In Revival" Foreword By Richard Owen Roberts (Gospel Folio Press, Canada; 2008).

12. "Olford On Scroggie: Stephen Olford's Notes on the Sermon Outlines of Graham Scroggie" Co-authored with Stephen Olford (The Old Paths Publications: www.theoldpathspublications.com).

13. "George Whitefield A Definitive Biography, Volumes 1 and 2 Combined"
(The Old Paths Publications:
 www.theoldpathspublications.com).

14. "George Whitefield A Definitive Biography In Two Volumes" (American edition published by Revival Literature, Asheville; 2012).

15. "God's Hitchhike Evangelist The Biography Of Rolfe Barnard" Foreword By Bob Doom (The Old Paths Publications:
www.theoldpathspublications.com).

16. "Asahel Nettleton Revival Preacher" Foreword By John Thornbury, Preface By Richard Owen Roberts (The Old Paths Publications:
www.theoldpathspublications.com).

17. "Sermons For Revival" (The Old Paths Publications: www.theoldpathspublications.com).

18. "A Noble Company Biographical Essays on Notable Particular Baptists in America Volume 11: Portrait of Rolfe Barnard" (Particular Baptist Press, Springfield; 2018).

19. "Lectures On Revival For A Laodicean Church," (The Old Paths Publications, www.theoldpathspublications.com)

20. "Sam Jones, A New Biography" (The Old Paths Publications: www.theoldpathspublications.com)

21. E. A. Johnston's Book Set, (The Old Paths Publications, www.theoldpathspublications.com (30% off retail)

22. "Revival Trilogy, Three Volumes in One": 1. "Realities of Revival," 2. "Call to Revival," 3. "The Church in Revival," The Old Paths Publications, Inc., www.theoldpathspublications.com

23. "How to Have a Daily Quiet Time," the Old Paths Publications, Inc.,

www.theoldpathspublications.com
24. "Going Higher With God," The Old Paths Publications, Inc., www.theoldpathspublications.com
25. "How to Preach For Revival," The Old Paths Publications, Inc., www.theoldpathspublications.com
26. "Faith Lessons in A Dynamic God," The Old Paths Publications, Inc., www.theoldpathspublications.com
27. "The Man God Uses" The Old Paths Publications, Inc., www.theoldpathspublications.com
28. "Recovery of The Gospel" The Old Paths Publications, Inc., www.theoldpathspublications.com

Many of these books can be purchased in The Old Paths Publications Bookstore at a discounted price and where you will find "Sample Pages." Go here:

https://www.theoldpathspublications.com/Pages/BookStore.htm